Ripley's Believe It or Not!

Developed and produced by Ripley Publishing Ltd

This edition published and distributed by:

Mason Crest
450 Parkway Drive, Suite D, Broomall, PA 19008
www.masoncrest.com

Printed and bound in the United States of America

First printing
9 8 7 6 5 4 3 2 1

Ripley's Believe It or Not!
Unbelievable Stories
ISBN: 978-1-4222-3155-5 (hardback)
Ripley's Believe It or Not!—Complete 8 Title Series
ISBN: 978-1-4222-3147-0

Cataloging-in-Publication Data on file with the Library of Congress

PUBLISHER'S NOTE
While every effort has been made to verify the accuracy of the entries in this book, the
Publishers cannot be held responsible for any errors contained in the work. They would
be glad to receive any information from readers.

WARNING
Some of the stunts and activities in this book are undertaken by experts and should not
be attempted by anyone without adequate training and supervision.

Download The Weird

UNBELIEVABLE STORIES

www.MasonCrest.com

UNBELIEVABLE STORIES

Extraordinary events. Read about the most terrific tales. Discover the man who pulls snakes through his nose, the boy who fell from the eighth floor of a building and survived, and the most unbelievable facts about the Titanic.

Rusty Haight is the human crash-test dummy, and has experienced more than 950 crashes in the name of research...

TWITTER WINNER

Charlie Sheen collected one million Twitter followers in just over a day when he signed up to the site in March 2011, becoming the fastest tweeter to reach seven figures. Sheen gained 60,000 followers before even posting his first tweet; he now has over 10 million, but that isn't even enough to place him inside the top 20 celebrity tweeters.

VIRTUAL SHOPPING

The world's first virtual retail store has opened in a busy subway station in Seoul, South Korea, where all the goods on display are just pictures. Choosing from over 500 items, ranging from food to electrical goods, smartphone users download an app and make purchases by taking photos of the barcodes. They can order goods on their way into work and have them delivered when they get home.

EVERY 24 HOURS

- **300 BILLION**
  e-mails are sent

- **22 BILLION**
  text messages are sent

- **4 BILLION**
  videos are viewed on YouTube

- **500 MILLION**
  people log on to Facebook

- **250 MILLION**
  pictures are uploaded to Facebook

- **500 MILLION**
  tweets are sent

- **1.4 MILLION**
  pictures are uploaded to Flickr

- **822,240**
  websites are added to the Internet

A car transporter became stuck on a mountainside near Greimersburg, Germany, after its GPS had mistakenly directed the driver along a steep forest trail. It took a whole day to recover the truck.

GPS ERROR

Picture Room

Dutch artist Erik Kessels filled a room with photos after downloading and printing every picture uploaded to the photo-sharing website Flickr in a 24-hour period—that's over one million images.

LUCKY BREAK

A three-year-old boy had an amazing escape when he fell from the eighth-floor window of an apartment building in Beijing, China, but became wedged behind an air conditioner protruding from a window on the floor below. Trapped between the conditioner and the wall, he was unable to fall any farther and was rescued with nothing worse than a few scratches and bruises.

🅡 ASHES TOUR Deb Green from Vancouver, Canada, advertised on the classified ads website craigslist for volunteers to take a vial of her late parents' ashes around the world and to sprinkle them at major landmarks. As a result, their ashes are now sprinkled, among other places, in a fountain in Las Vegas, in a beer garden in Amsterdam, and at the base of the Eiffel Tower in Paris. Deb said Alice and William Green could never afford to travel but had always wanted to visit far-flung countries.

🅡 MARRIED HERSELF On November 6, 2010, Chen Wei-yih, a 30-year-old office worker from Taipei, Taiwan, got married to herself. She arranged the ceremony that was held at a hotel and witnessed by 30 relatives and friends to show she was confident and happy with who she was.

🅡 BEGINNER'S LUCK Just minutes into his first attempt at metal detecting, three-year-old James Hyatt, of Billericay, England, struck gold—in the form of a 16th-century religious locket valued at nearly $4 million.

🅡 PREMATURE AGING To demonstrate their commitment to growing old together, Zhang Jin, 25, and his fiancée Yao Zenni, 26, of Nanjing, China, had pre-wedding photographs taken showing them as an elderly couple battling against the cold. The pair wore makeup and dyed their hair gray to make themselves look 50 years older.

🅡 MERCY MISSION World-War-II German fighter pilot Franz Stigler allowed a heavily damaged American B-17 bomber to escape during a 1943 mission—and 46 years later he became good friends with Charlie Brown, the bomber's pilot.

🅡 UNDER-QUALIFIED The Italian government funded a Libyan man to attend a training program in Rome so that he could learn how to be an underwater frogman, only to discover that he couldn't actually swim. It was later revealed that the candidate was the cousin of the official tasked with choosing participants for training programs and had liked the idea of a vacation in Rome.

🅡 LUCKY NUMBERS Twice in the space of a month in 2010, Israel's biweekly national lottery drew the same six winning numbers—13, 14, 26, 32, 33, and 36.

🅡 POETIC JUSTICE U.K. filmmaker Martin Cassini defended himself on a charge of speeding to overtake a truck by pleading his case to the court in Barnstaple, Devon, in rhyming couplets. Despite his testimony in verse, he was fined £175.

🅡 CLEVER FELLER In May 2010, a man lost in the wilderness of Northern Saskatchewan, Canada, signaled for help by chopping down electrical poles. He was rescued when the power company came out to investigate the downed lines.

🅡 THAT'S PROGRESS! It took three years for the first U.S. mint to produce its first million coins. Today, the Philadelphia, Pennsylvania, mint can stamp out a million coins in 30 minutes.

🅡 GRAVE VOWS In May 2011, two couples held their weddings in a Chinese cemetery, exchanging their vows among the gravestones. Wu Di and his bride Yang Xi and Wei Jian and his bride Liu Ling, all of whom work at the cemetery, chose the unusual venue as a declaration of their intention to be together until death. The wedding procession to Yong'an Cemetery in Tianjin consisted of 26 decorated cemetery carts.

BIZARRE BIKERS

If you see a watermelon riding a bike, it's almost certainly the result of a Kazakhstan company that has designed a range of weird motorcycle crash helmets in such styles as a brain, a tennis ball, a cracked walnut, and a watermelon.

HOME LOVER A couple from Mestre, Italy, took legal action in a desperate attempt to force their 41-year-old son to leave home. The parents said their son had a well-paid job but refused to move out, preferring to have his clothes laundered and his meals cooked by his mother. Forty-eight percent of Italians between the ages of 18 and 39 still live at home.

WHEELCHAIR ROBBER Peter Lawrence, 71, robbed a San Diego, California, bank of more than $2,000 in 2010... while in a wheelchair.

TWO-TOED TRIBE Many of the Vadoma people, a reclusive tribe in western Zimbabwe, have only two toes on each foot.

FALSE FRECKLES Scottish prosthetic technology company Touch Bionics has introduced a highly realistic range of false limbs that feature freckles, hairs, and even tattoos.

CUSHIONED FALL In January 2011, a woman survived falling 23 stories from a hotel rooftop in Buenos Aires, Argentina, after she landed on the roof of a taxi, which broke her fall.

FOOD TATTOOS Chef Lauren Wilton of Toronto, Canada, has decorated her body in food-related tattoos, including a whisk, a fork and spoon, two garlic heads, dandelion greens, and a boar's head on a platter.

UNDERPANTS RUN On September 24, 2011, thousands of people stripped down to their underwear and ran through Salt Lake City in protest at what they considered the strict laws of Utah.

FLORIDA TATTOO A burglary suspect in Tampa, Florida, was arrested after his alleged victims recognized him from a facial tattoo on his left cheek—an outline of the state of Florida.

MARRIED ON THE RUN A couple from Houston, Texas, got married during the 2011 city marathon. David Upton and Molly Johnston started the race as boyfriend and girlfriend but crossed the finish line as husband and wife after pausing briefly at the 16-mi (26-km) mark to exchange their marriage vows in front of friends. The bride complemented her running cap with a small white veil.

Unbelievable Stories

The Odd couple

Ripley's ask

Husband and wife team Hannibal Helmurto and Anastasia IV have performed together in the incredible Circus of Horrors show since 2005.

Where did you meet each other?
Anastasia: We met in our local pub in Camden Town, London. I spotted Hannibal from across the room, came over, asked if I could stroke his ears, and six years later we are still stroking ears.

Explain your acts to us.
Hannibal: One of the things I do is I swallow a long sword, and then take a bow forward with the sword inside me. It's very important that you keep your posture quite straight otherwise you can easily cut yourself and I don't intend to do that.
Anastasia: Hair hanging comes from China, and was originally done by Chinese men. It is a dying art because it is so unpleasant and hurts so much. It takes a lot of training and a lot of willpower. The hair takes about 45 minutes to tie. You have to plait it like you plait a rope, and obviously there is a risk that it will come undone. We both do fire eating. It was one of the first things I learned to do, and it is still very popular.

Do you have any rituals?
Anastasia: We always try to have 5 seconds for a cuddle before we go on.

When you watch your partner perform, are you ever worried about the risks?
Anastasia: We are always a bit worried, because the acts we do in the Circus of Horrors always contain a high element of danger. Everything we do has a calculated risk—we have to know our anatomy, and how far we can push each other so we are always looking out for each other. But when I decided to marry Hannibal, I married him the way he is and I wouldn't like to change him for the world.

Turn
the page

They must be one of the world's oddest couples. He swallows swords, hedge trimmers, and umbrella handles while she hangs upside down and lifts 110-lb (50-kg) lead weights by just her hair.

Meet husband and wife Hannibal Helmurto and Anastasia IV who, since 2005, have performed with the Circus of Horrors, a bizarre rock-and-roll theater show featuring contortionists, demon dwarfs, knife throwers, and other weird and wonderful circus performers.

Hannibal, whose body is covered with over 200 tattoos, used to be a German tax inspector called Helmut Kirchmeier until he went to a circus and was inspired by a sword-swallowing act. He started practicing with a toothbrush before moving on to a coat hanger and can now swallow a blade attached to a revolving electric drill.

It's a dangerous occupation—in 2011, he tore a 4-in (10-cm) hole in his esophagus while swallowing a neon lightbulb. He felt a burning pain and was taken to the hospital.

The Odd

While there, he was unable to speak for two weeks and had to be fed through tubes for five weeks. However, he was able to start training again just 12 weeks after leaving the hospital.

Polish-born **Anastasia Sawicka** studied science before running off to join the circus at 18. She used to walk on sword blades but, for the last two years, she has specialized in hair hanging. Suspended upside down from a rope, she can use her hair to lift a 120-lb (54-kg) woman off the ground. She has also pulled a minibus weighing 70 times her body weight... with her hair. She strengthens her hair before each performance by spraying it with water, which makes it less likely to break. Even so, when she first performed her hair-hanging routine she cried because the pain was so intense.

Couple

Brave Hound

Vernon Swart from Stellenbosch, South Africa, was horrified when he returned home to find his dog Bella running around with a large knife lodged firmly in her skull. The six-year-old Alsatian terrier crossbreed had suffered the injury as she chased burglars away from the property, but incredibly she did not appear to be in any pain, and later recovered. The veterinarian who eventually removed the knife said the dog had been only a fraction of an inch from death.

R **FATED TO MARRY** Amy Singley and Steven Smith of Bushkill Township, Pennsylvania, were born at the same hospital on the same day in 1986—when their mothers shared a hospital room—and on June 12, 2010, the 24-year-olds married.

R **DANCING CARROTS** To pave the way for proposing to his girlfriend, Pang Kun persuaded 48 of his friends to dress up as giant dancing carrots in a shopping mall at Qingdao, China. He spent $15,000 on carrot costumes and they rehearsed their dance routine for two days. The idea was to attract the attention of Zhao Xinyu because orange is her favorite color.

R **BIRTH PATTERN** Emily Beard was born in 1997 in Portsmouth, England, at 12 minutes past 12 on the 12th day of the 12th month. Her father David had been born at 40 minutes past four on the fourth day of the fourth month, her mother Helen was born on the tenth day of the tenth month, her brother Harry arrived on the sixth day of the sixth month, and their grandmother Sylvia was born on the 11th of the 11th.

R **PARALLEL LIVES** Graham Comrie, 45, and Graham Cormie, 47, who live just 10 mi (16 km) apart in Scotland, look almost identical, are both professional photographers and married to redheads, and have two daughters, and Lhasa Apso dogs as pets. Both men celebrated their silver wedding anniversaries in 2011. People confuse them for each other all the time, and they get messages from each other's friends on Facebook.

R **MISS MAPLE** Using detective skills she had learned at a Junior District Attorney crime-fighting summer camp, 12-year-old Jessica Maple quickly solved a burglary at her late great-grandmother's house in Atlanta, Georgia—a crime that had baffled the police.

R **LIMPED AWAY** One of South Africa's most wanted criminals—due to stand trial in relation to 35 armed bank robberies—escaped from police custody by simply walking out of a Pretoria courtroom door... on crutches.

R **MISSING RING** Robert McDuffy, a firefighter from Wareham, Massachusetts, lost his wedding ring while fighting a house fire. However, luckily for Robert, the homeowner found the ring—11 years later—and returned it.

ACTING DOUBLE

Margaret Clark was an entertainer born with her twin attached by the head to her stomach. That was the backstory proclaimed at her performances at sideshows across the United States, but Margaret did not have a conjoined twin; indeed, Margaret did not actually exist. She was an act played by sideshow operator Billy Logsdon, who ran "Side Show Beautiful" out of Indiana in the 1940s. The unfortunate baby twin was merely a rubber "gaff" taped to Billy's belly. His face was covered because he played another character in his shows, a hermaphrodite, also thought to be a hoax, and he did not want to be recognized. "Margaret" would appear alongside Billy's other classic sideshow acts including sword swallowers, small people, and "The Human Pincushion."

R **"CASHIER NUMBER FOUR, PLEASE"** The voice of Terry Green is heard in the U.K. about 30 million times every month as his is the voice that directs customers at banks and post offices to the next available counter.

R **NO NAME** Maximus Julius Pauson of Pasadena, California, wasn't given a name on his birth certificate and went without an official name for 19 years.

R **IRONIC CRASH** On January 31, 2011, a driver accidentally crashed into the same Tampa, Florida, insurance office that provided her with car insurance.

R **LATEX MASKS** Robbers who stole $60 million worth of jewelry in a 2009 raid in London, England, reportedly hired an unsuspecting makeup artist to disguise their faces with liquid latex masks. The artist, who thought the pair were appearing in a music video, also changed their hair color and skin tone during the $700, four-hour session.

☒ **LUCKY FIND** When Reg Barker of Suffolk, England, bought a box of old postcards at a garage sale, he was amazed to find one of them featured a picture of his mother. He paid $4 for the box stuffed with more than 200 postcards in 2009. When he looked through them, he saw one of crowds celebrating Victory in Europe Day on May 8, 1945. There, dancing with Canadian troops in London's Leicester Square, were his adoptive mot___ ___d aunt.

☒ **JOB SEARCH** During 200___ ___009, a homeless, jobless Californian eco___ ___mics graduate landed 50 jobs in 50 different U.S. states in 50 weeks. In his search for work around the country, former financial analyst Dan Seddiqui became—among other things— a lobster fisherman, a jazz-band conductor, a TV weatherman, a syrup processor, and even a Las Vegas wedding planner! He said that his favorite job was as a bartender in Louisiana during the Mardi Gras festival.

☒ **WALL VAULTER** The U.S. military's research arm has devised a robot the size of a shoebox that can jump over walls 25 ft (7.5 m) high. The Precision Urban Hopper is a four-wheeled, GPS-guided remote control car fitted with a piston leg that can propel it over obstacles up to 60 times its own size.

☒ **FACIAL RECOGNITION** A Japanese company has invented a vending machine that uses facial recognition to recommend drinks to customers. The machine uses sensors to work out the age and gender of a customer and then suggests items based on that information, while also taking into account factors such as the time of day and the weather. When the first interactive drinks machine was introduced at a Tokyo train station, sales were three times that of its predecessor.

CRASH MAN

Rusty Haight is the human crash-test dummy. As director of the San Diego-based Collision Safety Institute, Rusty has experienced more than 950 violent vehicle crash tests at speeds of up to 54 mph (87 km/h), and taken 140 air bags to the face. A former police traffic officer, Rusty uses his unique car-wreck experience to research automobile safety and investigate and reconstruct collisions.

TRAIN TRACK TREATMENT

A risky remedy has recently grown in popularity in West Java, Indonesia. Locals believe that lying down on active railway tracks will cure various ailments. Participants remain on the tracks for as long as the speeding trains will allow, believing that electrical currents running through the lines are beneficial to their health.

R WEDDING MACHINE In 2011, Marvin's Marvelous Mechanical Museum in Detroit, Michigan, bought a new vending machine that enables couples to get married for just $1. Devised by British company Concept Shed, the AutoWed has a robotic voice that takes couples through their vows, at the end of which they either press one button for "I do" or another for "Escape." At the end, they get a wedding receipt and two plastic rings.

R SHOT ORNAMENT Called to a home in Kansas City, police officers shot an alligator twice in the head before realizing it was a garden ornament. It was only when the second shot bounced off the alligator that they realized it was made of concrete.

R DIG THE BRIDE! To save money on wedding cars, groom Zhang Zongqiang, who works for a heavy machinery company, used a fleet of six mechanical diggers to transport himself, his bride Ye Yuzi, and their guests to the marriage ceremony in Henan Province, China. The couple stood in the bucket of the lead digger, which was decorated with ribbons and balloons, and tossed candies to well-wishers along the route.

R DOUBLE DELIGHT Shop owner Ron Rea of Belle Vernon, Pennsylvania, sold himself a winning $1.8-million lottery ticket in November 2010—and as the seller of the ticket, he received an extra $10,000!

R STONES FAN In October 2010, police in Chennai, India, arrested a man for smuggling more than 2,000 diamonds and precious stones in his stomach.

R CASH JIGSAW After a Taiwanese businessman had inadvertently dropped the equivalent of U.S. $6,000 of banknotes into a shredder, justice ministry worker Liu Hui-fen put them back together in just seven days. The 200 New Taiwan $1,000 bills were each ripped into about 20 pieces, but by locating the Chinese character *guo* (country) on each bill and then working outward, she managed to complete the cash jigsaw.

R I DOOOOOOO Jason Jenkins of Stoke-on-Trent, England, proposed to his girlfriend Melissa Bowen by having her engagement ring delivered by an owl. Carrying a diamond ring in a pink velvet bag on its leg, Zulu the owl swooped from a perch and landed on Jason's arm.

THE TRAIN TRANSPORTING IRON ORE FROM INLAND MAURITANIA TO THE COAST IS OFTEN 1.5 MI (2.4 KM) LONG.

Surprise Cargo

When police in Bargteheide, Germany, stopped a van that was driving erratically, they opened the rear doors—and found a car neatly parked on its side in the back. It was the brainchild of two men from Kazakhstan who, after buying a Mazda 626, decided to save on the costs of shipping it home on a trailer by loading it into their van, placing a mattress beneath the car to stop its doors getting scratched on the floor of the van. The police confiscated both the van and the car until the pair found a proper transporter.

R LATE DELIVERY A postcard from a soldier serving in the British Army in World War I was finally delivered in 2010—94 years late. The loving message from 19-year-old Alfred Arthur to his sister Ellen did not reach her address in Norwich, England, until long after both of them had died.

R MEMORABLE DATES Tyler Ashton Marx was born in Meridian, Idaho, at 11.11 a.m. on 1/11/11 (January 11, 2011). His older sister was born on September 9, 2009—09/09/09.

R RICH PICKINGS Raffi Stepanian, with a pair of tweezers, made $450 a week by searching the pavement cracks of New York City for valuables. The former jewelry setter found diamonds, rubies, and even platinum and gold.

HOLD TIGHT!

This brave lamb was snapped hitching a ride on the back of his owner's motorcycle in Havana, Cuba, in early 2011.

GRUB PROTEIN The European Union is promoting the nutritional benefits of eating low-cholesterol insects in dishes such as scorpion soup and locust salad. Grasshoppers offer 20 percent protein and just 6 percent fat compared to lean ground beef's 24 percent protein and 18 percent fat. Crickets are said to be high in calcium, termites rich in iron, and a portion of giant silkworm moth larvae provides all our daily copper and riboflavin needs.

METRO BAN The French cheese Epoisses, once a favorite of the emperor Napoleon Bonaparte, has been banned on the Paris Metro because of its strong odor.

CHOPSTICK TRADE A lack of wood in China has led to a U.S. company, Georgia Chopsticks, producing two million pairs of chopsticks a day to export to the country. Until the shortage, manufacturers in China produced 63 billion sets of chopsticks every year.

BEAR FEAST On May 10, 2010, the Union Rescue Mission Shelter in L.A., California, served meals of donated game meat including elk, boar, antelope, and black bear.

ACQUIRED TASTES Exotic snacks offered for sale by vendors on Wangfujing Street, Beijing, China, include dried sea horses, silkworms, sheep's penis, giant grasshoppers, starfish, roasted sparrows, cicadas, and inside-out snakes.

HEAD WAITER The Japanese capital, Tokyo, is gaining a reputation for outlandish themed restaurants. The Alcatraz ER restaurant is styled after a prison hospital and has drinks served in a life-sized mannequin head.

ANCIENT SOUP In 2010, archeologists in China discovered what they think is a 2,400-year-old pot of soup. The liquid and bones were in a sealed, bronze cooking vessel near the city of Xian, which was China's capital for over 1,100 years.

1,000 FLAVORS Ice cream makers Matt and Mike Casarez sold over 1,000 different flavors of ice cream at Crook's Palace, Black Hawk, Colorado. Their more unusual varieties included "Wasabi Sesame," "Popcorn," and "Sweet Pea."

MUMMIFIED LARVA Mummified caterpillar fungus is served with chicken or pork in soups in China and Tibet to improve the flavor. The Thitarodes caterpillar feeds on the roots of a fungus that grows high up in the Himalayas, but the fungus reacts by invading the caterpillar's entire body, eventually killing and mummifying it.

EXPLOSIVE FISH Walu—or Hawaiian butterfish—contains a high level of waxy compounds in its tissue, which when eaten in large amounts can cause severe diarrhea. Native Hawaiians called the fish Maku'u, or exploding intestines. It is banned in Japan and Italy.

JELLY BRAIN

Online retailer Firebox sells gelatin candies in the shape of human brains. The life-sized Gummi Brain is a little over 7½ in (19.5 cm) long, weighs over 6 lb 10 oz (3 kg), and comes in bubblegum flavor.

HEALTHY SNACKS Kansas State University nutritionist Dr. Mark Haub lost 27 lb (12.2 kg) in two months on a junk food diet of chocolate bars, potato chips, cookies, pizza, doughnuts, and sugary cereals. Despite his diet of sugary, salty, and fatty processed food, his body fat and bad cholesterol levels both fell.

BREAKING THE MOLD To mark its centenary in 2011, U.K. chocolate manufacturer Thorntons created the world's biggest chocolate bar at its factory in Derbyshire. The giant bar weighed 12,770 lb (5,792 kg)— around six tons—and measured 172 sq ft (16 sq m). The mold for the bar was set up in the company's parking lot and it took more than 50 bucket-carrying workers ten hours to fill it with liquid chocolate and then another three days for it to cool off and solidify.

SUPERMARKET SURPRISE

Tesco, the U.K.'s leading supermarket chain, is opening stores across China, but the stock is a little different from that usually found on its shelves. Its store in Qingdao caters for local tastes by selling such items as chicken's feet, turtles, dried sea horse, and whole dried lizard! Soaked in a vat of rice wine, dried lizard is said to be a fortifying drink.

R EGGSTRAORDINARY Brian Spotts of Dacono, Colorado, balanced 900 eggs on end on the marble floor of a Hong Kong mall in March 2011. He practices egg balancing for half an hour daily and stresses the need for a light touch and the correct grip with the thumb and forefinger of each hand positioned at the top of the egg.

R ROBO-NOODLE Robots cook noodles for customers at a restaurant in Nanping, China. The restaurant owner, Fan Ming, paid $1,500 for the robots whose eyes and chest lights flash as they chop the noodles into boiling water.

R LONGEST LOG A team of 80 chefs in Shanghai, China, created the world's longest Christmas yule log, measuring more than 0.6 mi (1 km) long and more than five times the length of the previous record. It took 24 hours to make the log using 904 eggs, 2,304 lb (1,045 kg) of flour, 460 lb (209 kg) of sugar, 884 lb (401 kg) of bitter chocolate, and 75 lb (34 kg) of vanilla.

R STIR-FRY Using a custom-built, 14-ft-wide (4.27-m) frying pan, staff and students at the University of Massachusetts prepared the world's largest stir-fry. The 4,010-lb (1,820-kg) meal included 800 lb (363 kg) of chicken, 500 lb (227 kg) of onions, 400 lb (181.5 kg) of carrots, and 300 lb (136 kg) of broccoli.

MONSTER MUSHROOM

Picked from the wild in Shaanxi Province, China, this edible puffball mushroom weighed in at a whopping 10 lb (4.5 kg).

R TUNA RECORD The owner of a chain of sushi restaurants in Tokyo, Japan, paid a record $747,000 for a 593-lb (269-kg) bluefin tuna in January 2012, the equivalent of $106 for each piece of sushi.

R WINE FLOOD Workers at a liquor store in Sheboygan, Wisconsin, fled for their lives when a 78-ft-long (24-m) shelf collapsed, sending nearly 7,000 bottles of wine crashing to the floor.

R GOLDEN CHEESE Cheesemakers in Leicestershire, England, have made a Stilton cheese containing real gold. Clawson Stilton Gold is made from white Stilton infused with a mixture of edible gold leaf and real gold liqueur. The golden cheese sells for about $1,000 per kilo (2.2 lb).

R CUPCAKE TOWER Volunteers in Vereeniging, South Africa, baked 21,000 cupcakes that were then arranged into a vast tower 19 tiers high and 11 ft 9 in (3.6 m) wide.

Chinese Treat

The slippery sluglike marine creature the sea cucumber (or sea rat) is a popular delicacy in Chinese cooking. It is considered an aphrodisiac and is used in medicine to treat everything from high blood pressure in humans to joint pain in pot-bellied pigs. The dried ovary of the sea cucumber is eaten in Japan and is called *konoko*.

TITANIC

Titanic under construction at the Harland and Wolff shipyard in Belfast, Ireland. The deck sat 60 ft (18 m) above the waterline.

At the time of her launch, the luxury liner *Titanic* was not only the biggest ship in the world but also the largest movable object ever built. Yet, she made only one voyage, in April 1912, which ended in disaster. Over one hundred years later, the story remains as compelling as it is chilling.

After setting off from Southampton, England, the New York-bound *Titanic* struck an iceberg in the dead of night in the North Atlantic and sank in the early hours of April 15, with the loss of over 1,500 lives. Out of the estimated 1,523 people who perished, only 328 bodies were recovered, of which 128 were unrecognizable. The temperature of the water was only 28°F (−2°C) and most passengers would have died of hypothermia or heart attacks. Over 62 percent of first-class passengers on the *Titanic* were saved, compared with just 25 percent of those who traveled third class.

Although only 12 sq ft (1.1 sq m) of the *Titanic*'s hull was gouged open by the collision, the design of the ship meant that a little over 2½ hours after impact, the supposedly "unsinkable" vessel disappeared beneath the waves.

The last *Titanic* survivor, Millvina Dean, died on May 31, 2009. She was just nine weeks old at the time of the tragedy, the youngest passenger on the ship. Her father died on the *Titanic*, but her mother and brother survived.

Ship workers in the Belfast shipyard are dwarfed by one of *Titanic*'s three propellers, measuring almost 24 ft (7.3 m) across.

The Titanic newspaper coverage shown here is from the *Daily Express*, Friday, April 15, 1932.

GREAT SEA TRAGEDY RECALLED IN NEW PICTURES

1932 — Twenty Years

APRIL 15! Twenty years ago to-day the mighty liner Titanic sank on her maiden voyage, with the loss of more than 1,500 lives.

Most of these pictures, now published for the first time, were taken by Father Browne, a Jesuit priest, who travelled in the ill-fated ship to Queenstown. Above is the scene on Waterloo Station before the boat-train left, with Colonel J. J. Astor, one of the victims, facing the camera.

The £2,000,000 liner, then the largest ship in the world, left Southampton on April 10. Twenty minutes before midnight on April 14 she crashed into a submerged iceberg and sank in less than three hours; a tragedy unparalleled in the history of sea-passenger service.

TWO of the first-class passengers.

LUNCH in the magnificent dining saloon.

IN THE GYMNASIUM.—Mr. McCawley, the physical instructor, and Mr. Pow, the electrician, both lost their lives.

FAREWELL.—The last glimpse of the Titanic from the coast of Ireland.

"SPARKS," Mr. Harold Bride, the liner's wireless operator. He was saved.

SURVIVORS arriving alongside the Carpathia. Left: The last message received from the doomed ship.

PASSENGERS on the second-class deck on the promenade.

THE FACTS

- **It cost $7.5 million to build**—the equivalent of $400 million today
- Each of the **engines was the size of a three-story house**
- **The four funnels were 62 ft (19 m) high and 22 ft (6.7 m) in diameter**, wide enough to drive two trains through
- The hull was constructed with **three million rivets**
- The **center anchor weighed 15.5 tons** and needed 20 horses to pull it through Belfast to the shipyard
- The ship contained more than **200 mi (320 km) of electrical wiring**
- The ship was lit by **10,000 lightbulbs**
- *Titanic*'s whistles could be heard from a distance of **11 mi (18 km) away**
- The ship was fitted with 29 boilers and 159 furnaces, and carried more than **8,000 tons of coal**
- **16,800 gal (63,645 l) of drinking water** were consumed on board every day
- If the 882-ft-long (269-m) ship had been stood on its end, it would have been **taller than any building in the world at that time**
- **Sixty chefs** and chefs' assistants worked in five kitchens providing food for the passengers

One of the last SOS telegrams sent from the *Titanic* before it sank.

The iceberg that hit the *Titanic* towered about 75 ft (23 m) above the surface of the ocean, approximately the height of a seven-story building. As 90 percent of an iceberg's mass is usually below the surface, it could have extended a further 400–600 ft (120–180 m) underwater.

WEALTHY PASSENGER The wealthiest passenger on board was U.S. businessman Colonel John Jacob Astor IV, who owned a large chunk of Manhattan and whose personal fortune was estimated at $150 million. In today's money, that equates to $102.2 billion, enough to make him the richest man in the world. He did not survive the disaster.

TRAVELING LIGHT? The luggage of wealthy Philadelphian Billy Carter included 60 shirts, 15 pairs of shoes, 24 polo sticks, and a new Renault car! Everything, including the car, went down with the *Titanic*, although Carter himself survived.

MISSED THE BOAT At least 55 passengers canceled their bookings on the *Titanic* at the last minute and 22 crew members also missed the boat. They included three brothers, Bertram, Tom, and Alfred Slade, who had been taken on as trimmers in the coal bunkers, but stopped for a last-minute drink in a Southampton pub and were prevented from boarding the liner after being delayed by a passing freight train.

DYING VISION In Scotland on the night of April 14, 1912, a dying girl named Jessie predicted to Salvation Army captain W. Rex Sowden the tragedy that would occur three-and-a-half hours later. She spoke of a big ship sinking, people drowning, and someone called Wally "playing a fiddle and coming to you." Among those who drowned on the *Titanic* was bandmaster Wallace Hartley, whom Sowden had known as a boy but had since lost touch with.

UNIFORM BILL No members of the *Titanic* band survived, but the Black Talent Agency of Liverpool who hired the musicians sent the family of violinist Jock Hume a bill for $3.50 for the cost of the unpaid and unreturned uniform.

No human remains have ever been discovered on or around the wreck of the *Titanic*. Any bodies that sank with the wreck have been eaten by fish and crustacea. All that remain are the shoes and boots of the victims still lying on the sea floor.

Titanic memorabilia, including a pocket watch recovered from the wreck that stopped one hour after the ship sank.

Realizing they would not escape, U.S. mining magnate Benjamin Guggenheim and his valet changed into full evening dress, reappearing on deck to declare: "We've dressed up in our best and are prepared to go down like gentlemen."

LOST PROPERTY

Among passengers' insurance claims submitted to the White Star Line following the sinking were:

- Personal property **$177,352.75**, Charlotte Drake Cardeza
- Oil painting **$100,000**, Hakan Bjornstrom-Steffanson
- Renault 35 hp automobile **$5,000**, Billy Carter
- Signed picture of Garibaldi **$3,000**, Emilio Portaluppi
- Champion French bulldog **$750**, Robert W. Daniel
- Four roosters and hens **$207.87**, Ella Holmes
- Set of bagpipes **$50**, Eugene Daly

On board were 13 couples celebrating their honeymoons.

More than 5,000 artifacts, including china dishes from the dining rooms, have been removed from the wreck of the ship.

The wreck of the *Titanic* was discovered on September 1, 1985, by underwater explorer Robert Ballard. It lay largely intact at a depth of 12,000 ft (3,660 m) below the surface of the Atlantic off the coast of Newfoundland. This depth is six times deeper than a human diver has ever descended, and enough to crush human lungs. Using a small submersible craft, Ballard explored the wreck in 1986, but it wasn't until August 1998 that a section of the hull was hauled to the surface.

SHIP'S STORE

- **75,000 lb (34,000 kg)** of fresh meat
- **25,000 lb (11,400 kg)** of poultry and game
- **11,000 lb (5,000 kg)** of fresh fish
- **40,000** eggs
- **36,000** oranges
- **16,000** lemons
- **20,000** bottles of beer
- **1,500** bottles of wine
- **40 tons** of potatoes
- **1,500 gal (5,700 l)** of fresh milk
- **12,000** dinner plates
- **8,000** cut-glass tumblers
- **45,000** table napkins
- **15,000** pillow slips
- **25,000** fine towels
- **18,000** bedsheets

R UNKNOWN IMPOSTOR The mother of Southampton fireman Thomas Hart was distraught to learn that he had gone down with the ship... only for him to return home a month later in perfect health. A drunken Hart had lost his discharge book in a pub, and an unknown impostor had taken his job and had paid for his duplicity with his life.

R GIRL POWER With insufficient men to propel her lifeboat containing 28 people, first-class passenger Margaret Brown of Denver, Colorado, took off her life jacket, and began rowing. Her efforts inspired some of the other women to lend a hand and led to her being immortalized by Hollywood in *The Unsinkable Molly Brown*.

OVER-THE-TOP

Arturas Zuokas, mayor of Lithuania's capital city, Vilnius, surprised bystanders when he drove over an illegally parked vehicle in a Russian armored personnel carrier, crushing the vehicle beyond repair. The elaborate stunt was a headline-grabbing response to luxury cars being parked illegally in the capital.

WOODEN SCOOTER Carlos Alberto, a carpenter from Portugal, built a functioning replica of a Vespa motor scooter almost entirely from wood.

TIGHT SQUEEZE In December 2010, 26 members of the New York City-based Pilobolus Dance Company squeezed their bodies into a standard MINI car.

PAPER PLANE In October 2010, near Madrid, Spain, a paper airplane fitted with a tiny camera was launched into space to photograph its descent to Earth. For Operation PARIS (Paper Aircraft Released Into Space), it was attached to a weather balloon. When the balloon burst 17 mi (27 km) up, the plane began to fall, taking pictures on its way.

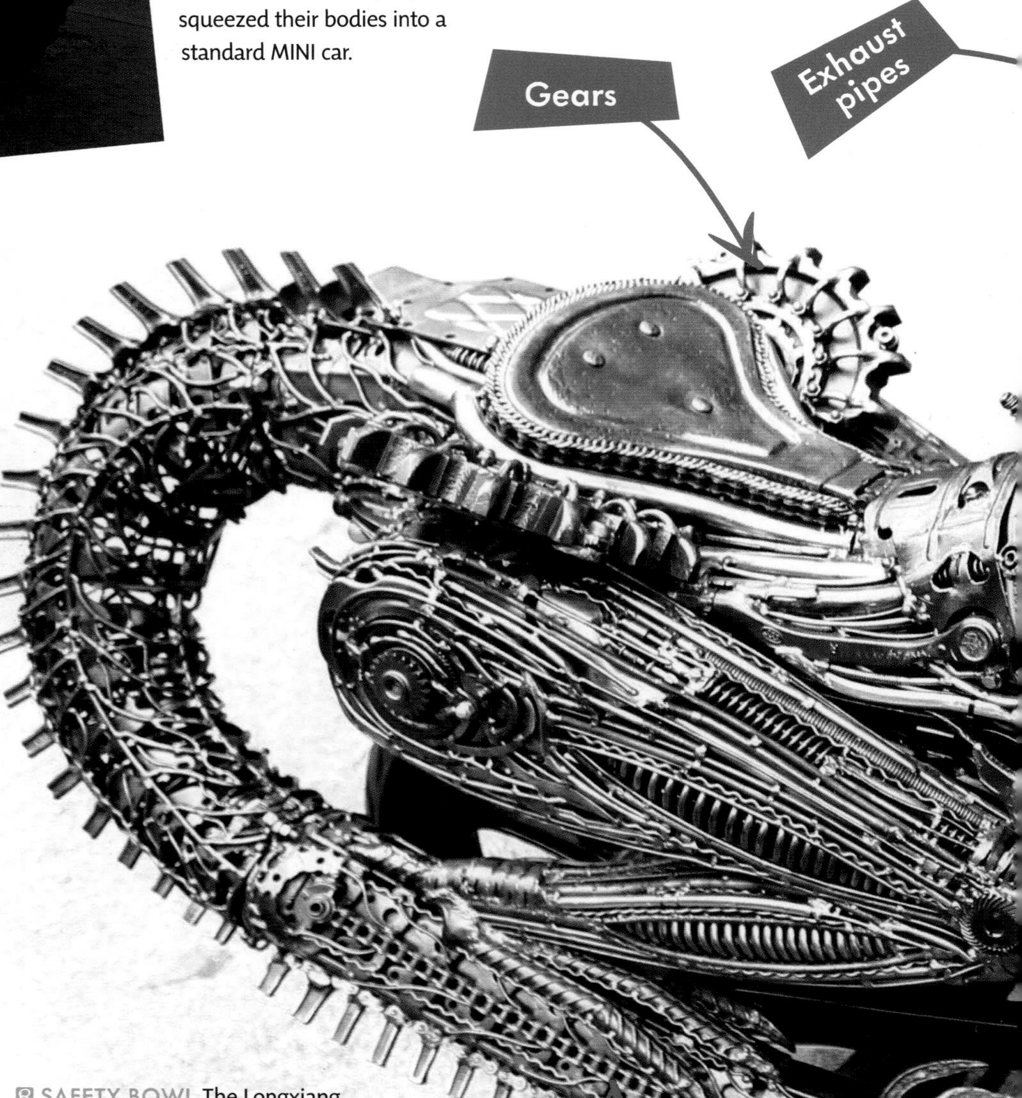

Gears

Exhaust pipes

Bike chain

MINI MINI Retired mechanic Lester Atherfold from Napier, New Zealand, trimmed over 2 ft (60 cm) off his 1964 MINI car so that it could fit into the trunk of his motor home. He reduced the 10-ft-long (3-m) MINI to 7 ft 10 in (2.4 m) by slicing a chunk from the middle, narrowing the chassis, and fitting a new sub-frame, transmission, clutch, and dashboard.

ARMORED CAR The "Popemobile," the Roman Catholic Pope's touring car, is armored with 3-in (8-cm) blast-resistant glass panels and has its own internal air supply for protection against a chemical or biological attack.

QUICK THINKING Duane Innes of Kent, Washington State, deliberately crashed into a truck driven by 80-year-old Bill Pace. The crash stopped Pace's truck, saving his life after he had passed out behind the wheel.

SAFETY BOWL The Longxiang Public Bus Company in Changsha, China, uses a hanging bowl of water in its buses as a visual reminder for drivers to drive calmly and carefully.

STRANGE HYBRID Motorbike-crazy Markus Sell, from Jonschwil, Switzerland, welded the rear half of a Renault Clio car onto the front half of a motorbike. But, as he roared along at 70 mph (115 km/h), police stopped him and claimed the vehicle was unsafe.

Unbelievable Stories

Bike chains

ALIEN BIKE

It looks like an alien monster, but it's really a motorbike. This stunning creation was assembled by artist Roongroina Sangwongprisarn at his workshops in Bangkok, Thailand. Roongroina builds crazy-looking motorbikes from the recycled spare parts of cars, motorcycles, and bicycles—and his awesome metal sculptures can actually be ridden.

Springs and cables

FAMILY RUN Competing in the London Marathon on April 17, 2011, 52-year-old Kelvin Amos and his son Shane, 31, from Stoke-on-Trent, England, finished in a combined time of 6 hours 3 minutes 7 seconds—the fastest-ever father-and-son team to run a marathon.

SNAKE CHALLENGE In 2010, David Jones, a 44-year-old carpenter from Crawley, England, spent four months locked in a room with 40 poisonous snakes, including cobras, black mambas, and puff adders, in Johannesburg, South Africa.

MOVIE STATUES Dave Bailey of Middlesex, England, has collected *Star Wars* memorabilia for over 30 years. His £60,000 hoard includes full-sized statues of all the main characters, including a 7-ft-tall (2.1-m) Darth Vader.

WING WALK On November 15, 2010, pensioner Tom Lackey from Birmingham, England, broke his own record as the world's oldest wing walker— at the age of 90. He was strapped to the 32-ft-long (9.7-m) wing of a plane and flown 500 ft (152 m) above the ground in Gloucestershire.

DELAYED DIPLOMA Eighty-six-year-old James Livingston from Savannah, Georgia, graduated from Screven County High, and was awarded his high-school diploma, on May 28, 2010. His parents had allowed him to leave high school in 1942 to help fight World War II on condition that he earned his diploma when he got back.

JAIL BREAK On August 22, 2011, exactly 25 years after he first performed the stunt of escaping from Waushara County Jail, Wisconsin, Anthony Martin, the "King of Escapists," repeated the feat—and in almost half the time. Despite being placed in a straitjacket, strapped to a ladder, and locked behind four steel doors, he was able to complete his escape in just 2 minutes 50 seconds—nearly two minutes faster than in 1986.

ISLAND SWIM Julie Bradshaw from Loughborough, England, swam the 28.5 mi (45.9 km) around New York's Manhattan Island in 9 hours 28 minutes, using only the butterfly stroke.

TONGUE TWISTER

China's Li Jinlong used his mouth to balance a tower of three plastic bottles, 12 wine glasses, five glass plates, and 16 soccer balls, and then made the entire tower spin using only his tongue. His tongue had to support and spin a total weight of 33 lb (15 kg).

TOILET MUSEUM In Wiesbaden, Germany, toilet fan Michael Berger has opened a museum devoted exclusively to the lavatory. The unusual attraction contains his personal collection of toilet brushes, toilet roll holders, and toilet seats. Among the extraordinary artifacts are a "Mona Lisa" toilet roll holder, a Virgin Mary toilet brush holder, and a urinal with Adolf Hitler's face on the inside, which was designed after World War II to show disapproval of the Nazi regime.

HEAVY LOADS

On August 27, 2011, 11 former U.K. servicemen climbed England's highest peak with 100-lb (45-kg) tumble dryers or washing machines on their backs. It took the ex-marines and paratroopers eight hours to climb up and down the 3,209-ft-high (978-m) Scafell Pike.

CHANNEL SWIM At the age of 70 years 4 months, Roger Allsopp, a retired surgeon from Guernsey in the Channel Islands, became the oldest person to swim the English Channel when he completed the 24-mi (39-km) crossing from Dover, England, to northern France in 17 hours 51 minutes on August 30, 2011.

BIKE LEAP Chilean base-jumper Julio Munoz roared off a massive cliff in the Andes on his motorbike, free-falling around 3,000 ft (915 m) before opening his parachute. It took him three years to plan the spectacular stunt, during which he had several cameras attached to his body so that he could film the jump from different angles.

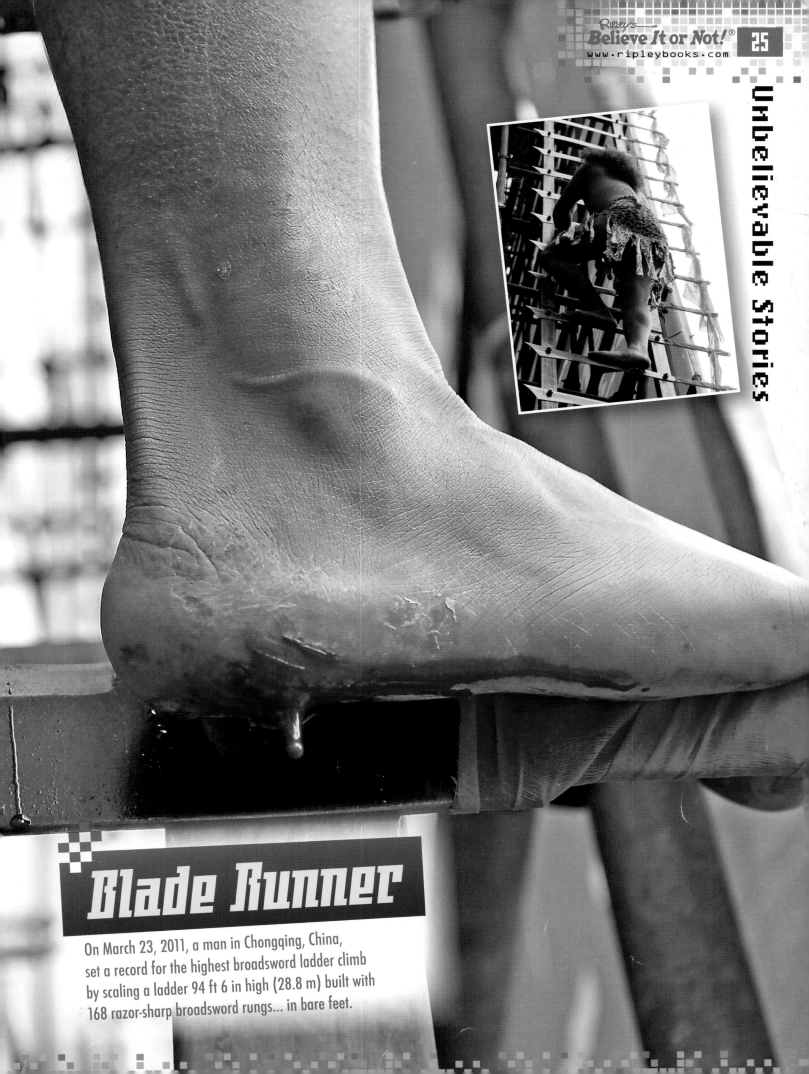

Blade Runner

On March 23, 2011, a man in Chongqing, China, set a record for the highest broadsword ladder climb by scaling a ladder 94 ft 6 in high (28.8 m) built with 168 razor-sharp broadsword rungs... in bare feet.

Fowl Food

Grilled, stewed, or fried, a plate of duck tongues is considered one of the most luxurious snacks in parts of the Far East. Devotees of the dish say it's the faint hint of meat, the paper-thin layers of cartilage, and the pockets of fat that make the tongues so delicious! The taste of the tongues, barely 2 in (5 cm) long, is like no other duck meat, and the texture is much more creamy. Those who need further convincing might try this recipe for duck tongues—fried.

Fried Duck Tongues

2 tsp soy sauce
1 tsp rice wine, such as sake or Shaoxing
½ tsp white pepper
chili sauce or cayenne pepper
1 lb (450 g) duck tongues
½ of 1 egg white, beaten
1 tbsp cornstarch
2 cups oil

1. *Combine the soy sauce, rice wine, white pepper, and a dash of chili sauce in a bowl. Add the duck tongues and mix evenly. Leave them in the marinade for 30 minutes.*

2. *Remove the duck tongues from the mixture and transfer them to another bowl. Add the egg white and cornstarch to the tongues and mix.*

3. *Pour the oil in a wok and heat to 350°F (175°C). Gently slip the duck tongues into the oil and stir to prevent sticking. Deep fry for about 2 minutes, until cooked through.*

RICE CRAZY There are more than 40,000 different types of rice in the world. The Chinese alone eat 130 million tons of rice every year.

STINKING BISHOP After the highly pungent Stinking Bishop cheese—made on a single farm in Gloucestershire, England—was mentioned briefly in the 2005 Oscar-winning animated movie *Wallace & Gromit: The Curse of the Were-Rabbit*, demand for it rose by 500 percent.

SAUSAGE ADDICT David Harding from London, England, has spent nearly £2,000 on counseling and hypnosis to try to beat his addiction for eating an average of 13 sausages a day. The 47-year-old has eaten at least one sausage a day since he was five and spends up to £700 a year on sausages.

JESUS IMAGE Toby Elles of Salford, England, fell asleep while frying bacon—and woke up to find a lifelike image of Jesus Christ, complete with long hair and beard, burned into the pan.

TOP DOG In honor of National Hot Dog Day, on July 23, 2011, the Brockton Rox baseball team of Massachusetts created the world's most expensive hot dog, selling for $80. The dog was deep fried and rolled in truffle oil, then coated with porcini dust, sprinkled with white truffle shavings, and topped with crème fraîche, caviar, and roe before being served in a buckwheat blini roll.

TASTEFUL HOTEL

During the holiday season in December 2011, the Fairmont Hotel in San Francisco, California, put on display a gingerbread house of epic proportions. Constructed out of 7,500 home-baked gingerbread bricks and 1,200 lb (544 kg) of royal icing, the 23-ft-high (7-m) house was decorated with 650 lb (295 kg) of colorful candies and featured a special room where children could write a letter to Santa—with express delivery to the North Pole.

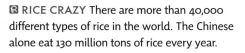
view from inside the house

RED HOT CHILI Chili grower Nick Woods of Grantham, England, has grown a new chili, Infinity, with a heat that measures 1.17 million on the Scoville Scale that grades chili heat. That's 300 times hotter than Tabasco sauce, and so hot it carries a health warning. When he first tasted it raw, he was unable to speak or stand up, shook uncontrollably, and felt physically sick.

VEGETABLE KING Gardener Peter Glazebrook from Nottinghamshire, England, set a new record for the world's heaviest onion when he exhibited a monster weighing just under 18 lb (8.1 kg) at the Harrogate Flower Show in 2011.

NONPROFIT CAFE In 2010, the Panera Bread Company opened a nonprofit café in Clayton, Missouri, where customers just pay what they can afford and those who are unable to pay can volunteer their time.

RARE MALT A rare 3-pt (1.5-l) bottle of single malt Scotch whisky sold for $460,000 at an auction in New York in November 2010. The 64-year-old Macallan malt had been bottled in a one-of-a-kind, handcrafted crystal Lalique decanter.

MICRO BREWERY Bragdy Gwynant, a brewery in Capel Bangor, Wales, is located in a former outhouse and is only 25 sq ft (2.3 sq m) in size. It brews ale for just one customer—the Tynllidiart Arms inn next door.

PRICE OF BREAD At the height of Zimbabwe's economic collapse in 2008, it cost 700 million Zimbabwean dollars to buy a single loaf of bread.

RAVISHING RATS

Finger-licking-good rats are rounded up and sold at almost $1.70 a pound ($3.80/kg) in the markets of Canh Nau, Vietnam. Formerly a food eaten through necessity in times of poverty, the rodents are now a popular, local specialty.

TACO LINE As part of the 2011 Phoenix Phestival in Oregon, a group of taco engineers took just 15 minutes to build a line of tacos measuring 177 ft (53.9 m) long.

SHRIMP COCKTAIL More than 80 chefs in Mazatlán, Mexico, joined forces to concoct the world's largest shrimp cocktail, weighing 1,187 lb (538.5 kg). It was served in a dip containing 127 lb (58 kg) of ketchup and 22 lb (10 kg) of lemon juice.

PERFECT PIE A £3,000 mince pie—the most expensive in the world—went on display in London, England, in 2011. Made by chef Andrew Stellitano from a 17th-century recipe, the mince pie included high-grade platinum leaf, holy water from Lourdes to bind the pastry, vanilla beans and cinnamon from Eastern spice markets, and ambergris sugar harvested from sperm whale secretions.

PRIZE PUFF At the 2011 Wisconsin State Fair, a team of bakers created a cream puff that weighed a whopping 125.6 lb (57 kg). The prize puff measured 7½ in (19 cm) high and 38 in (96 cm) wide.

TINY CAMERA U.S. catalog company Hammacher Schlemmer has introduced the world's smallest fully functional digital camera—which is no bigger than a human fingertip. The tiny camera measures just over 1 in (2.5 cm) in all dimensions and weighs only 0.5 oz (14 g).

BEACHED WHALE A dead 33-ft-long (10-m) whale was found in a field in Yorkshire, England—half a mile from the sea. It became stranded after being carried to shore by an exceptionally high tide while it was hunting.

SHARED HUSBAND Undecided whether to marry for love or proceed with an arranged marriage to a bride chosen by his family, Azhar Haidri found a solution by marrying both women in the space of 24 hours at Multan, Pakistan, in October 2010. Both brides—21-year-old Rumana Aslam, and his family's choice, 28-year-old Humaira Qasim—were happy to marry the same man.

FIRST-CLASS MALE Chester Arthur Reed, aged 95, of Riverside, California, retired from his job as a U.S. postal worker after 37 years with nearly two years of unused sick time.

TOILET TANTRUM A man who owns a toilet tissue roll that was once rejected by The Beatles has been offered $1,500 for a single sheet. The Liverpool, U.K., band refused to use the paper while recording at London's Abbey Road studios in the 1960s because it was too hard and shiny and had the name of record company EMI stamped on every sheet. The roll was bought at an auction by Beatles fan Barry Thomas for $120 in 1980.

This photo of young Louis Quinnell was taken with a pinhole camera fitted in the back of his dad's mouth! Justin Quinnell from Bristol, England, positioned the film in his mouth so that his back teeth could keep it stationary, and then held his mouth wide open to take the pictures. He created the pinhole camera by placing tinfoil over a pinprick one-fifth of a millimeter wide on the cartridge, and used it to take unique mouth's-eye pictures of the world around him, including the Sydney Opera House in Australia and more everyday occurrences such as taking a bath. Sometimes he had to stand still with his mouth open in front of his subject for a minute to ensure that the film was properly exposed.

WASTE OF MONEY The U.S. Bureau of Printing and Engraving produced more than a billion $100 bills for release in 2011 that were rendered worthless when a machine improperly creased the bills during printing.

HARD TO SWALLOW Australian sword swallower Chayne Hultgren, who once swallowed 27 swords simultaneously, was arrested in 2011 while performing before a large crowd in a New York City square—for brandishing a sword in public.

ON TIME All three children born to Lowri Dearsley of Manchester, England, have arrived at precisely the same time, 7.43. Overcoming incredible odds, daughter Ella was born at 7.43 a.m. on October 10, 2005, another daughter, Evie, was born at 7.43 p.m. on December 26, 2007, and a son Harrison was born at 7.43 a.m. on January 20, 2011.

WHERE THE STREETS HAVE NO NAME About 100 street signs mysteriously disappeared from the town of Northborough, Massachusetts, in the first six months of 2011.

100-FT GEYSER When a car smashed into an L.A., California, fire hydrant in 2011, shearing off the top, the broken hydrant sprayed a fountain of water 100 ft (30 m) into the air, flooding streets and causing people to be evacuated from their homes.

INVISIBLE BEGGAR Fed up with being ignored by passersby, street beggar Nemanja Petrovic from Subotica, Serbia, tossed his cap and shoes down on the sidewalk with a handwritten card saying "Invisible Beggar" and abandoned his pitch. He returned to find his cap full of money—so now he puts down the card and a pair of shoes as a prop and goes to a nearby café while the donations pour in.

BANANA ATTACK A costumed gorilla mascot at a cell-phone store in Strongsville, Ohio, was attacked in July 2011—by a banana. The store manager reported that a boy dressed as a banana emerged from bushes and leaped at the man wearing the gorilla suit. The banana split before police arrived.

RED ROSES Xiao Wang, a groom in Qingzhen, China, spent a year's salary buying 99,999 red roses for his 2010 wedding to Xiao Liu—because in China the number nine is considered lucky. The flowers had to be flown in from the other side of the country and were delivered to the wedding in a fleet of 30 cars.

SPECIAL PEN Bangladeshi businessman Dr. Moosa Bin Shamsher has a 24-carat gold ballpoint pen, encrusted with 7,500 diamonds, which he uses to sign only business deals worth $10 million or greater.

RING REUNITED Joan Spiers was reunited with a diamond ring that she had flushed down the toilet two-and-a-half years earlier. Following the mishap—at a hotel near Gatwick in Surrey, England—she hired a waste firm to search 12,000 gal (54,500 l) of sewage for the ring, but to no avail. Then, by coincidence, an employee from the same firm stumbled across it 30 months later at a sewage works.

TUSKS SEIZED In January 2011, a court in St. Petersburg, Russia, confiscated 3 tons of mammoth tusks—64 full and 14 reconstructed—from a criminal gang that had been trying to smuggle them out of the country. The tusks came from Siberian mammoths and had survived for thousands of years because of the permafrost that covers most of the region.

DUTCH SHARE Dutch student Ruben Schalk found an early share of the Dutch East India Company in the archives of Hoorn, Netherlands. The company was disbanded more than 200 years ago, but the share is still worth over $750,000 to collectors.

DEMOLITION DERBY Seventy-seven-year-old Marlies Schiller caused over $200,000 damage to five brand new cars in a showroom while she was trying to take one out for a test drive. She shot backward and forward across the Volkswagen garage in Apolda, Germany, smashing into everything in her path, her trail of destruction ending only when she crashed through a window and hit a car parked outside.

LONGEST INTERVIEW Australian radio presenter Richard Glover set a world record for the longest-ever radio or TV interview when he talked to journalist and author Peter FitzSimons for 24 hours in a Sydney studio.

TWINS PEAK Among the 34 employees on duty at the Bexley Park Pool, South Euclid, Ohio, in the summer of 2011 were four sets of twins (including two identical sets), meaning that nearly a quarter of the staff were twins.

RED TAPE Although he has been living in America for almost a century, 95-year-old Leeland Davidson of Centralia, Washington State, discovered in early 2011 that he wasn't officially an American because his parents did not fill out the proper paperwork.

BANK PARTY On June 2, 2011, June Gregg celebrated her 100th birthday with a party at the Huntington National Bank branch in Chillicothe, Ohio—where she still held the same savings account her father opened for her in 1913.

BANNED NAMES Among baby names that have been banned in New Zealand in recent years are Yeah Detroit, Keenan Got Lucy, Fish and Chips (given to twins), and Talula Does The Hula From Hawaii. Believe it or not, however, Number 16 Bus Shelter was permitted.

WET GUESTS Eva and Pavel Jaworzno got engaged and married underwater. Their August 2011 wedding ceremony took place in a flooded open-pit mine in southern Poland, diving with 275 guests, making it the world's largest underwater wedding.

JACKPOT JOY Four workers from the Bell Canada call center in Scarborough, Ontario, who were members of a syndicate that won a $50-million Lotto Max draw in January 2011, were also part of a group of Bell employees who won $1 million in 2007.

BOTTLE MESSAGE Paula Pierce's father folded a message into a bottle and put it in the ocean at Hampton Beach, New Hampshire. More than 50 years later, it turned up 2,000 mi (3,200 km) away on the Turks and Caicos Islands in the West Indies and was returned to Paula.

MONSTER WOMBAT In 2011, paleontologists in Queensland, Australia, uncovered an almost complete skeleton of a diprotodon, a prehistoric wombat-like creature the size of an SUV car, that was the world's biggest marsupial. The three-ton monster, which had large tusks but a tiny brain, became extinct about 35,000 years ago.

ROBOT MARATHON At the world's first robot marathon—raced around 423 laps of a track in Osaka, Japan, in February 2011—the winner completed the 26-mi (42-km) course in just over two days at an average speed of 0.48 mph (0.77 km/h). At the finish, the winning robot—16-in-tall (40-cm) Robovie-PC—waved its arms and bowed to the crowd.

MILLION-DOLLAR BOTTLE For the woman who wants to smell like a million dollars, DKNY created a million-dollar bottle of perfume. Their special bottle of Golden Delicious fragrance was carved from polished 14-carat yellow and white gold. Covered in 2,700 white diamonds and 183 yellow sapphires, it also has a flawless single diamond in the bottle cap.

STEEL CAGE April Pignatoro and Michael Curry married in Riverhead, New York State, on June 6, 2010, in a steel cage placed underwater in a shark tank.

NOT AGAIN! Two years after being ticketed for speeding in London, England, a man emigrated to Christchurch, New Zealand, and was again booked for speeding—by the same police officer who had stopped him in England! Like the disbelieving driver, Constable Andy Flitton had recently moved to New Zealand.

WEED WHEELS We could soon be driving cars or riding bicycles with tires made from weeds. A species of dandelion—*Taraxacum kok-saghyz* (TKS)—produces molecules of rubber in its sap, and scientists at Ohio State University are conducting crossbreeding experiments in the hope of increasing the rubber yield from the plant so that it can be used commercially.

Grennan envisages the synthetic sweat glands being installed on at least three different types of industrial robot—a bomb disposal robot, a surgeon robot, and an industrial picker robot. On the bomb disposal robot, it would release the smell of human fear, which has been proven to enhance a person's cognitive performance. On the picker robot, the gland would release a chemical called androstadienone, which is found in male sweat, and, if dispersed on an assembly line, could improve the performance of nearby female workers. The surgery robot would release a mist of oxytocin, a chemical found in the human brain, which, when breathed in through the nose, causes people to become more trusting. So meeting the robot before surgery should increase the patient's trust in the operation.

SWEATY ROBOTS

U.K. designer Kevin Grennan has created robots with sweaty armpits. He has augmented three existing robots with "sweat glands" made from Japanese artificial sweat, a product used to test fabrics for sweat stains. In response to a chemical stimulus, each robot targets a specific form of human subconscious behavior—fear, focus, and trust—to improve its effectiveness.

TREBLE CHANCE Believe it or not, Jennifer and Driss Allali from Eastbourne, England, have three children with the same birthday—Najla, Adam, and Sami were all born on October 7, in 2005, 2007, and 2010 respectively.

BANK ERROR While renovating a former bank in Ghent, Belgium, as a base for his accounting firm, Ferhat Kaya opened an old safe that had been left behind by the previous owners and found bags of 20 and 50 euro bills, totaling around $380,000.

HUMAN COW Scientists in Argentina have created a cow that produces "human" milk. By incorporating two human genes into the cow before birth, scientists from the National Institute of Agribusiness Technology in Buenos Aires have developed an animal that will produce milk similar to that of humans.

SPACE LESSON People who spend long periods of time in space have to relearn to place objects down rather than letting go of them in midair.

MICROSCOPIC FROG A computer sciences professor at a university in Nanchang, China, has artificially bred a tiny species of frog that can be seen clearly only through a magnifying glass. Hu Gansheng's frogs are just 0.2 in (0.5 cm) long but can leap 4 in (10 cm)—20 times their body length.

DIAMOND PLANET Astronomers believe they have discovered a planet that contains large amounts of diamond 4,000 light-years away. The planet, which is about 37,000 mi (60,000 km) wide—over five times the diameter of Earth—is thought to be the remains of a once-massive star in the Milky Way. Its high density indicates that it must be made of crystalline carbon—in other words, diamond.

ARTIFICIAL BRAIN Scientists at the University of Pittsburgh, Pennsylvania, created a tiny artificial brain that demonstrated 12 seconds of short-term memory. The microbrain was derived from rat brain cells and grown in a petri dish.

BACON CLOCK California-based inventor Matty Sallin has devised an alarm clock that wakes you up with the smell of bacon. Wake n'Bacon turns on ten minutes before you are due to wake up and slowly sizzles frozen slices of bacon beneath two halogen lightbulbs. Its built-in fan then wafts the aroma of cooking bacon around the room to wake you up gently.

Snake Twist

For over 30 years, Liu Fei of Jiangxi Province, China, has been pulling 3-ft-long (0.9-m) snakes through his nose, sometimes even using two snakes simultaneously. His most unnerving moment came when he accidentally swallowed one of the snakes, but luckily for Liu it died in his stomach before it could cause any harm.

ROBOT SAFETY Robot-driven cars created by the software company Google have traveled more than 140,000 mi (224,000 km) on U.S. streets with only a single accident. The cars use artificial-intelligence software that can sense anything near the vehicle and mimic the decisions made by a human driver. Engineers say that robot drivers react faster than humans, have 360-degree perception, and do not get distracted, sleepy, or intoxicated.

BUTTER BLUNDER In May 2011, a visitor to Boijmans van Beuningen museum in Rotterdam, the Netherlands, accidentally trod in an artwork made of peanut butter. He absentmindedly wandered onto Peanut Butter Platform, a piece by Dutch artist Wim T. Schippers that was acquired by the museum in December 2010. It features 290 gal (1,100 l) of peanut butter—enough to fill more than 2,000 regular-sized jars.

FERRARI FAN Jon Ryder of Sheffield, England, loves his yellow 1996 Ferrari 355 Spider so much he parks it in his living room. He drives it through a garage door at the end of the room so he can admire it from his sofa.

WRONG TURN A British man and his wife drove their Renault into the side of a church near Immenstadt, Germany, after obeying faulty instructions from their GPS. The couple ended up in the hospital with minor injuries, their car was wrecked, and $30,000 of damage was done to the church—all because the GPS directed them to turn right where there was actually no road.

HEAVY LOAD A truck carrying steel pipes that increased its total weight to 98 tons was so heavy that it fell through a bridge and landed in a river. The truck was being driven across the Dongrong Bridge in Changchun, China, when the road suddenly collapsed beneath it, leaving a truck-sized hole measuring 46 x 16 ft (14 x 5 m).

KEEP TURNING California's Ridge Route mountain highway—built in 1915 and linking Los Angeles to Bakersfield—has 697 turns in just 36 mi (58 km) of road.

SINGING MICE Japanese scientists have created mice that can sing. By tinkering with a mouse's DNA so that it randomly mutated, they have managed to develop more than 100 mice that can chirp like sparrows.

METAL MARRIAGE

Elaine Davidson, who has nearly 7,000 body piercings, got married in June 2011 to Douglas Watson... who has none. At her wedding in Edinburgh, Scotland, only her face was visible—and that was painted with bright colors and covered in 192 piercings.

FLOATING VAN An amphibious ice-cream van toured Britain's seaside resorts in 2011. Driven by Dave Mountfield from Brighton, Sussex, HMS Flake 99 had a top speed of five knots and chimed Rod Stewart's "Sailing" as it took to the water.

Index

Page numbers in italic refer to the illustrations

Unbelievable Stories

ACKNOWLEDGMENTS

Front cover (b) Courtesy of The Fairmont Hotel; **4** Rusty Haight, The Collision Safety Institute; **6** (t) AP Photo/Chris Pizzello, (b) Park Ji-Hwan/AFP/Getty Images; **6–7** Caters News; **7** (c) © Picture Alliance/Photoshot; **8** Quirky China News/Rex Features; **9** (l) good.kz/Rex Features; **12** (t) Miller & Maclean; **12–13** (b) Rusty Haight, The Collision Safety Institute; **14** (t) Reuters/Enny Nuraheni; **15** (t) © Europics, (b) Franklin Reyes/AP/Press Association Image; **16** (t) Wenn.com, (b) Sinopix/Rex Features; **17** (t) Quirky China News/Rex Features, (b) Matthew Holzmann; **18** (t) PA Archive/Press Association Images, (c, b) Library of Congress; **19** Getty Images; **20** (t) Getty Images, (b) Les Wilson/Rex Features; **20–21** © Ralph White/Corbis; **21** (r) © Ralph White/Corbis; **22** (t) Zilvinas Abaravicius; **22–23** Reuters/Sukree Sukplang; **24** (l) Quirky China News/Rex Features, (r) Tim Stewart News/Rex Features; **25** Imagine China; **26** (t) Reuters/Paul Yeung, (c, b) Courtesy of The Fairmont Hotel; **27** Reuters/Kham; **28–29** Justin Quinnell; **30** Kevin Grennan; **31** Imagine China; **32–33** Danny Lawson/PA Archive/Press Association Images; **Back cover** Matthew Holzmann

Key: t = top, b = bottom, c = center, l = left, r = right, sp = single page, dp = double page

All other photos are from Ripley Entertainment Inc.
Every attempt has been made to acknowledge correctly and contact copyright holders and we apologize in advance
for any unintentional errors or omissions, which will be corrected in future editions.